73

The Way We Move Through Water
and other poems

ଓ

by Lino Anunciacion

Write Bloody Publishing
America's Independent Press

Los Angeles, CA

writebloody.com

Anunciacion, Lino.
1ˢᵗ edition.
ISBN: 978-1938912900

Cover Design by Tyler Lavoie
Interior Layout by Winona Leon
Proofread by Florence Davies
Edited by Ebony Stewart

Type set in Bergamo from www.theleagueofmoveabletype.com

Printed in the USA

Write Bloody Publishing
Los Angeles, CA

Support Independent Presses
writebloody.com

For Tamir,
You deserve so much more than these pages.

For Alisha and Xavier,
I'll pave the way, you take it from there.

For The Golden Bodies,
Keep your shine. Keep your joy. Keep going.

THE WAY WE MOVE THROUGH WATER

The Way We Move Through Water

1.
Navy

2.
Violet

3.
Gold

I, like so many of you, am now looking to get my Joy back, after it ran away to a more deserving land than this.

—Hanif Abdurraqib

1.
NAVY

I was born by the river | in a little tent | Oh and just like the river, I've been runnin' ever since | It's been a long time coming | but I know a change gonna come

| oh yes, it will.

—Sam Cooke

WATER IS THE PRAYER

I don't pray the way I used to | mostly silence | mostly tears | but this is original prayer | the first words | a sacrificial ritual | I give you all the salt | and water | in my body | and in return | I come up clean |

I don't understand why I need to speak | for you to hear me | when all I know of you is silence | unfamiliar with your voice beyond the words of passing strangers | did you really speak of light | when you poured water over the salt | of the earth | and said | that it | was good | or was it | all in | your head |

I too | have sent my love in the form of silence | but never in the form of floods | if crying is the ritual | water is the prayer | but I don't feel clean | and neither should you | | amen |

GODWATER

A widow in the making rubs
a wet cloth against her husband's feverish skin.

A barista dips their burnt finger tips
in a glass of melting ice.

A hurricane washes away a confederate
statue made of copper.

A storm pulls the loose petals
from a cherry blossom tree.

Blood drips from the edge
of a searing exit wound.

The Sun can still be seen on
the edge of a rain cloud.

The restorative forces of water
can still be considerably dangerous

an overdose | or |
conceptually | a flood

I | too | have choked on what I believed
would heal me.

Sent the holiest things down
the wrong pipe.

I | too | have put too much
faith in rain.

If god is in | the water,
I am both thirsty and drowning.

If god is in | the water
I am swimming the wrong way.

LEMONADE

I'm holding a wet towel to your forehead
pouring cold water over your palms.
America, you were the second woman I ever loved
the first creature I ever wanted to hold in my hands
since I was old enough to know of want and hold
I dreamed of small flags and ovals and stars
I dreamed of a million ears pressed against my chest
a country of people, all certain that I was still breathing

but look at us now
holding on to old lovers
reminiscent of a life you once lived
our fingers on your fading pulse
decaying photos on the wall of
a time when we were happy
but they are so unfair and unfamiliar to me
I have always been rubbing your screaming temples
loving you has always been unlearning
fighting for you with your hand at my throat—
what an absolutely devastating way to treat the ones
who love you
what a wicked song you force me to sing

but here I am, singing.

Fourteen Black Birds, Mid-Prestige

I.
fourteen black birds land on the
Capitol steps in Washington, D.C.
all at once, they disappear in the night
and no one wakes up until mourning.
a nation places black feathers in
their hair and goes about their day.

II.
a police officer pretends to be a magician.
a precinct shifts into a top hat.
look at the empty holding cell.
look at the flying coffins, LOOK:
America's greatest disappearing act;
works well with dead bodies.
works better with
dark
skin.

III.
a black bird washes its wings by a pool in Texas.
a magician drags a black bird by its beak
presses it into his top hat with his palms.
a police officer grabs a black bird by its wings
and bends them backwards.

IV.
a magician reaches into a top hat
and pulls out
    a bird feather
    a tombstone
places them behind your ear
pulls out
    a vacation
    a check
    a rug

V.
you watch a flock of black birds fly
into the horizon and
you go about your day;
nothing to see
here.

VI.
but the magic trick ain't finished
until the prestige takes place
until what has vanished
reappears
and every day
you watch a flock of black birds fly
and ain't that just like a black bird
to always show up when there's
black bird magic
to be had.

GHOSTSPEAK

Some nights | the ghosts of the KKK visit me in my sleep | they
teach me how to build a fire | they say |

you can take the white cloaks, you can take the whips and rope. |
we'll always come back. Maybe this time in blue, maybe this time
with guns. | you can get rid of the name but you cannot get rid of the
chains. some fires grow too large | to lay down. and you can smell
a black boy burning | a hundred miles away. | it smells equal part
honey and copper | like the penny sized bullet wounds | like the bee
sting | you can learn a lot about somebody from how fast they go up
in flames | you can learn a lot about somebody from the God that
they pray to. what stories they fear the most. how many black boys
have turned to piles of salt? | ash | sugar | dust | how many black
boys looked back while they were running away? why do you run?
don't you appreciate the God that we gave you? don't you want to be
holy? | black boy, heaven looks good on you | why don't you pray
to it. | why don't we send you there | don't you know | we are a
religious people | but if we must be the sinners, someone must be the
lamb | black boy, your blood tastes like old testament | black boy,
your blood don't got no mercy in it. | the first cavemen had skin like
yours. they discovered fire before they ever found Christ. the first
thing they burned was their fingertips. black boy, you've been on
fire ever since. we keep burning you and you always resurrect. black
boy listen, your whole family is a forest of acacia's, your whole body
is a burning bush. we hear God talking to us through the flames. boy
don't you get it. you ain't ever heard of fire up in heaven. there is
only one place in which they speak of flames.

HOW TO BUILD A FIRE

a stone's throw away from the body | a river made of sticks and mud and mud. pour salt on the skin for leverage | a mother weeping sticks like a waterfall. | feed the river. | unbury the body from the ice and rub the frost off the bones. | | | | | | | | I'm telling you this is an old trick boy, just focus. | now listen | | you hear that? | beehives | we hide them in the pockets. | they make good bait because they don't swim good | but god damn what a good fire | black boys make good firewood | they burn slow | sit still boy I'm trying to teach you something | some people just want to see the world burn | as ambitious as that may be | look at all this firewood | you and yours, the copper keys | me and mine, the thunder | the snap after the firework | the smoke beneath the nest | the honey spills out of the body | or perhaps, gasoline | flammable as it may be.

First We Must Shed the Skin

First, I shed my skin
and I shed my skin
and I shed my skin
until

> the parts of me that remember are
> completely dismembered

or

> I feel clean. Unscathed, unbloodied,
> brand new in my golden body.

until

I unwrap this skin and let the past fall out
I unhinge this jaw and let the sad pour out
I unmask myself and let my self come out

and then I shed my skin.
and then I shed my skin.
and then I'm the nobody I always wanted to be.

GOLDEN BOY, UNREST

The taste of copper on my tongue,
golden jaw, golden boy;
I grit my teeth in my sleep.

I rise from my sleep with sweat on my brow.
There are | | ghosts, bleeding and crowded upon my shoulder.
I wake up with bruises I can't explain.

They walked into heaven the same way.

Burning Monks

every fire
pulls from the wood

every fire
still reaches for the sun

we all want to go home
safe travels, degradation

every fire fades away quietly
eventually, every fire moves slow and falls asleep

we all want to die from natural causes
we just don't know what that means

Again, We Must Shed the Skin

It is far too
    heavy.
    tight.
    human.

I will
    shed my skin.
    become undone.
    leave traces of myself in the crevices of the world.

I will
    go the distance.
    seek the great echo.
    find Oceanus.
    put him to rest.

I want my feet to taste all the wonder there is to offer.
I want to forget where I came from.

I will
    carry my ghosts to bed.
    rest them next to Oceanus.
    kill the loneliness
    and shed my skin.

I want a new body,
so I will get rid of what's holding this one together.

I want an unhaunted vessel,
so I will show my ghosts the way out.

I want peace and quiet,
so I will finally put the sea to sleep.

THIRTEEN WAYS TO LOOK AT A HANGING TREE

1.
How its boney fingers press into the velvet of the night sky.
How it caresses the sun out of its slumber
and everything turns purple and soft and gentle.

2.
I want you to cut me open.
I want my loved ones to count the rings.
I want to wrap around their fingers
like ghosts holding hands.

I wish to die and
return as a cherry blossom every time.
I wish to blossom and fade like so many before me
I don't want anyone to find it normal.

3.
The old slaves inside me are dead (or nearly dying)
and | after they cut me open | I want to pull them out.
They all hold hands like monkey
in a barrel
or
a tree.

I want to wear them like wedding rings
on my boney fingers
or hang them like strange fruit from my limbs
I want to eat with my hands.

4.
Why does my lover flinch when I wake her in the morning?
Why does she hold my hand as we walk through the forest?

5.
I admire the tree that holds the body.
How it reaches for God's hands
and the moon kisses its palms and prays for this to cease.

6.
I know the tree fears death as much as I do.
I feel it shiver
while it holds me.
Reaches its hand out firmly
into the night and whispers no to the darkness.

7.
The slaves inside me are dying.
They reached their hand out and whispered
no to the darkness.

8.
From a distance,
I see birds taking flight
shaking the leaves on their way out.
Perhaps the trees flinch when the Sun says good morning,
and strange fruit falls from the shivering limbs
like wedding rings off of severed fingers.

9.
It will not fall far. It will grow a forest.
A forest of hands reach
for the only God they're allowed to believe in.

10.
A forest of slaves is dying inside me.

11.
I want to be cherry blossom.
perhaps I am willow.

12.
The Sun rises on a dark forest and a whole village flinches.
Slaves are dying inside of it.
They press their hands into their loved ones, tell them to
never be afraid of the dark.
They drifted away, wading into the
horizon they would eternally look into
and shiver.

13.
My ancestors drifted here on a tree,
or perhaps what used to be.
Pressed their bony fingers into it,
as it shook from the waves.
Walked, hand in hand, chain in chain,
to the hesitant shore.
Cringed at the sunlight and the whisper
of a new world.

I can still taste the fruit when I wake.
I can hear the clang of chains like a handful
of wedding rings, spilling to the floor.

2.

VIOLET

I feel like it's just me | Look
I feel like I can't breathe | Look

I feel like the whole world want me to pray for 'em | but who the
fuck prayin' for me?

—Kendrick Lamar

THE LANGUAGE OF FLOWERS

says that Daisies grow absolutely
anywhere.

I wonder if they grow in
Ferguson | Baton Rouge
Charlotte | Charleston.

I wonder if someone mistook those
Daises for the trees they used to hang us from.

I wonder if the Daisies in those cities weren't white
enough, so they painted them red. I think about the
parents that stopped growing Daisies and started
burying them instead.

I wonder if Mother Earth speaks The Language.
She has to—with so many daisies buried inside her,
all those petals she must sing to sleep every night.
What does she have to say about all this deforestation?
What does God have to say about all this genocide?
I would ask, but I would never bother
two parents in mourning.

I imagine God crying
in an attempt to water all of his gardens—
so confused as to why they keep cutting us down.

Rock Me Real Slowly

America   look at me
I am unhinging my jaw at the edge of the Mississippi River
swallowing the flood
admonishing the grief
I've got sterling silver around my wrists
the pain of my people coalesce into
an existence known as me and
I sit at the edge of the gulf
and I float along with the rest
and I pray to a God who swam
through the universe before
turning the lights on
and I am wondering how many
bullet holes keep a body from floating
I am asking God which sinners
he lets into heaven
I am wondering if Trayvon
will ever run into his bullet wounds
in the kingdom of the Lord
I am burying my head in the delta
I am asking you   America
if you ever think
if you ever wonder
about whether the black bodies you send
home early   arrive at heaven's gate
in the same condition they were delivered
are the exit wounds fresh   or
is dried blood cleaned
from floating downstream

An Apology

this is the part where I apologize   the truth is a
venomous forearm
begging to remain unharmed   but I must draw the
blood I must
be honest with you   for every Trayvon
Martin there is
an unfamiliar name and   an unfamiliar body
for every Sandra Bland
there is a ghost that I refuse   to make eye contact
with   sometimes
I wonder if Tamir wasn't the first   would I remember
his face would I keep his favorite color boy   if I could
carry you all   with me I promise that I would
          burdens have torn
at my rotator cuffs   I would   let the guilt eat at my
flesh if it made more space for
you   tell me how   my gratitude for
survival   is synonymous with me
being thankful that   my shoes are my shoes
and your death is yours
being alive is a microaggression   how dare my shirt
say   I can't breathe
if I still have the means to do so   when one of my
lungs is filled with grief and the other
collapsed with guilt   how loud can I scream
hands up don't shoot
when the only police officer   to point a gun at me
          got an emergency call on his radio
when I put my palms to the sky   am I reaching for
yours to bring you back down or am I holding the door
shut   to be alive feels like a protest and a
cop out
most days I wish it was me   and I know you're
somewhere thinking that they want to be us until it's time
to be us   and I know that black bodies
occupy all the shelf space

in the Kingdom of the Lord
to life than death
I just don't know their names
you on my shoulders
I just don't have the

and I know there's more

and I would carry

space.

How Do You Grow Up Older Than Someone Who Died

after Hanif Abdurraqib

a youth poet loses their best friend a summer ago
asks me, how do you grow up older than someone who died
and I am cotton-mouthed for a moment
tongue dried by my Uncle PeeWee who's
however-many-years-old-had-things-gone
differently

but

you do so aggressively. you carry this life in your fists
like a light you cannot let go of just yet and
when it feels like the end, you ask for one more
and when it feels like the end, you just keep going
you carry their energy within, you never let them forget
hide their name between your teeth and your bottom lip
someone has to live the life that they were meant to be
so let them be the energy that carries your feet and find
them in what little light is left in this world
because you have to. because they need you to. they can't
kill us until they kill us and they can't die until we die.

GRIEFWATER

Once, I was a small child
waist-deep in the Gulf of Mexico and
my mother was on the shoreline
begging me to swim
as red flags flew up in the air
and what have I learned so far:
there are always sharks in the water
both of substance and of my own creation
and there is always a way out of the grief
as long as there's a voice to follow back home.

BLINK

and all of a sudden you're twenty-two and you drink your coffee
black and you're a hundred feet away from your grandmother's
deathbed and you look like an extra in a movie or a tv show about
doctors like maybe it's scrubs or greys anatomy but there's no music
just you a cup of black drip and a body that knows not what to do
with where it stands. and simultaneously it feels as though you
cannot think past what exists within this temporary space and yet you
feel as though you could fit into the palm of some gentle hand and
this is the beginning of grief, a stretching and a shrinking, something
left unsettled and someone you love three floors above you with the
cold wind grazing its wanting fingers over her tongue.

THE WAY WE MOVE THROUGH WATER

a drop of water
moves slowly
down the
shower wall

a black body
braces for | | impact
and then steps
into the | rain

the way we move through water like
the captain
navigating grief:
unsure of how many bodies lie beneath us.

a glass of water
melts on the
kitchen table

a nervous hand
taps against
the wood

our mother's eyes
never leave the door frame

the way water swims down black
bodies unsure of the
way to our roots

the way our mothers can smell a storm
from fifty miles | away

the way it rains both
bullets and | | bodies
in America

our mothers
are the only
evacuation plan

their arms,
the only safety net
we've ever known

but what net
do you know
to be bulletproof

what arms can
withstand the oncoming
storm

our bodies
still smell like
rain
and it is phenomenal

how the whole
house floods
when we don't | | come home

how the faucets
pour endlessly
between our mothers'
eye
lids

how there is always
a broken pipe
of wind or water

how some day
is the last day
we say our mothers' name
how some day always comes
unpredictable as it may be.

the way we move through water,
you think the blood is thick as honey

the first shower
you take
after seeing
a dead body
will smell like sea salt and copper.

the third dead body
they wake up to
won't wash
off for two days.

the way we move through water,
unsure of when the sinking begins,
not quite ready for the abyss
when it comes.

A Portrait of My Mother and Her Mother

a body running purely | off the energies of forgiveness. | a desperate
attempt at a good thing | you | cupping your palms around the petals
of a dozen roses | crisp flowers in the wake of a tragedy | cut off
by the stem | a silent room disrupted by my shaking hands on fine
china | she runs her hands through your hair | my grounded heels |
shivering knees | this body on the other side of the glass | the steam
from a terrible cup of coffee | in a hospital cafeteria | the dust of our
loved ones that we collect | and carry with us | in us | the only thing
I have buried is this anger | and it is digging its way back into my
heels | scratches on my ankles | can't remember | the time or place
| of the last time I said I love you | but I do remember laughter | you
| walking up the stairs | she says | it's time for you to come home |
and at the time | I knew that you were | but not in the way we could
walk away clean with | the heart stops beating | in a slow decline |
you were the only one who loved her more than me | and I don't
know how to do this alone

Roadkill, Nightmare

Usually, she is dead on impact. By the time we get out of
the truck, if we start there, the medics roll her out on a
stretcher in a body bag—a leather casket filled with
broken glass and dried blood.
Sometimes I wake up right then and there; sometimes I
stand on the precipice of the sidewalk and cry until the
ocean of my own creation carries me back to shore.
In some dreams my mother and sister bury her in the back yard or
the living room—sometimes I wake up to the
bad news | | sometimes it's really her
but sometimes it's someone else's | face | | someone I
loved or someone I really knew.
How many stories my head can make about someone I
never knew but will always remember. I wake up with
lockjaw and phantom limbs for teeth
I shudder at crosswalks; how much I laughed when she
says I talk in my sleep; how much I would've said if I
could've spoken in that moment or in my dreams.
| | In my dreams, my most real ones, I am standing on
the sidewalk. A woman drunken-stumbles on the corner.
The lights flash green. I grab her arm.
She smiles at me, bright and becoming, before walking
away. | | One thousand eyes. Five hundred
open mouths. A scream. A cry in the distance.
Her shoes go flying and I wake up with her in my teeth.

HONEYWATER

You are the bees | disappearing at a dramatic pace. | This country
| the doves, rinsing the oil from their feathers | Your blood is the
honey | and it spills everywhere | it sticks on everything | a viscosity
that does not move well down our throats | Your mother will scream
when she sees you on the concrete. | There is nothing you could
| | | | | | do | | | | | | | | | | | | | It's almost as if we don't have a | | | | | | | | |
choice | | | | | | It's almost as if this is how it has to be.

3.

GOLD

*You gotta move slowly | take and eat my body like it's holy |
I've been praying for you.*

—Jamila Woods

LET'S KEEP GOING

the sand from the hour glass falls directly into my mouth
this is a direct result of my refusal to accept the fact that
we all must die. I am begging you to keep going   I
am swallowing all the mistakes you made I am giving you
a second chance   look at me

you are the direct result of fifty-fifty shots falling right where
we need them you with your hands and all the king's men
deserve to carry sand instead of mountain tops listen I
want something lighter for you because I swear to God if
I let go now you would just float away

I want to thank you for the recipes to sadness and grief
for the tears that ran down my face from my eyes and
dried before they ever reached the floor   even now
you have dug your teeth into the softest spots of my palms
even now you ask more callouses from me and I kindly refuse

if I turn the hourglass over does that mean I can return to
my grandmother's bed can I make good on my promises or
deliver one more I love you don't you think you've asked
 enough of me don't you think I deserve a little more time

no. how can you ask for more when there's still blood in
the water. even now the bees lie dead in the snow. Thaw
 out the honey that was frozen in your bones. feed all the
things you love in this life let them eat it from your hands.
let them kindly refuse.

I am   begging you to keep going. I am   giving you a
second chance. you   with your hands and all the honey
in the world. me with my jaw pressed tight against
the glass. you don't need more   time you just need
to keep going. I kindly   refuse to let you give up on
this. I kindly refuse to die with sand in my mouth.

GOLDEN BOY, AS SEEN BY THE BLUES

Hi my name is Golden Boy and I'm | a good man | the song
bird of a generation | the last of the real ones | Hello my name is
Golden Boy and I'm | the American dream | a stone at the bottom
of the river | what happens when the builder refused | the last of
a generation who were raised by a generation that grew up on the
blues | you know | my father knew a man named B.B. | who would
whisper to a guitar and make it sing on key | I'd do the same thing
to the river | to the lake | whatever body of water that wished for
a name | Hi my name is Golden Boy and a boy with my face |
died with skittles in his mouth | spilling tea into the harbor | and I
wonder where the old heads found the rhythm to dance | to sing | to
go without mentioning the grief | the water | the wading | I wonder
how the ghosts creeped into the chorus line | how the vocal chords
work | in the dark | I want to know how they opened their mouths
| without regurgitating | a flock of crows | how busy the process of
swallowing first | how dare we create in a world that decays us | such
talent bred into our skin | how sweet the honey that bleeds from the
trunk of a dying thing

GOLDEN BOY, AS SEEN BY THE DOVES

for frank ocean

golden jaw, golden boy;
speak gold into their ears.
speak bold, brazen
make them dance,
make them dance.

Black boy, orange channel
blonde hair.

Black body, blue bruises
golden shoes.

Black suit, black shades
golden tongue.

golden jaw, golden boy;
spit gold into their mouths.
spit poet, speak poet,
make them eat you
make them taste you

Black boy turns gold for
more gold and the whole world
goes blind.

Black boy gets stuck
between ivory teeth

Black boy turns into golden plaque.

Black boy turns blue
in the moonlight and swims
good in the wake of a song, his lungs
are too gold to sing sweetly or swim
out of.

black boy, blue bruises
golden gate.

heaven looks good on you, boy.
go ahead and sing to it.

golden jaw, golden boy;
spit at the gates of heaven.
spit boy, speak boy.
make God cry.
ask God why.

YOLANDA

I turned my grandmother into a bundle of lavender
I keep her at the foot of my bed   I toss and turn and we
do not share space well
and most mornings I wake up early enough to put her
back together before leaving for the day I am most certain
that if I grow something with her
name in mind then she can never die

I am confident in my abilities to carry dead weight
it is as simple as staring out the driver side window and
here lie the violets after which she was named and
here lie the roses she once brought me and
here lie our fingers covered in sticky rice and
every so often there is a ringing in the silence and
this is where I have buried her
where only I can see
this is where she has become
a part of me

and one more thing before you go:
my best memory of you   standing at the bottom of
the stairwell of my mother's home. you, laughing in your
lavender blouse on your way up to your room
if I had known you weren't coming back down
if I had known you were on your way home
I would've kept you laughing right next to me
I would've followed you up the stairs.

THE SEA IS NOT YOURS

The Sea is not
> your lover
> your mother
> your homecoming

and you don't have to drown to learn as much.

Why do you stare at the horizon
like
> home is a journey and not
> the rebirth you've been looking for
like
> every single renaissance is out there
> and for so long you've been
>> decaying
>> reneging
>> on your promise
>> of More.

God's paint is dribbling at your ankles
rubbing against your sacrificial shins,
whispering to the oil inside your body
to come out and play.

You look at that horizon
like
> you want to unravel but
> the tide has never been strong enough

like
> you want to go somewhere
> and never come back

and you want to trade all those Bad Words
for just one Good Bye

so you
        hang them from your palms,
        hold them above your head
        wade out into the canvas,
        until you're
                clavicle deep
                in the holy
then you
        wait for the good one.
        the sunrise.
        the tidal wave that takes you back
        to shore

and it never comes.

LAMELLOPHONE AND THE GULF

I will do everything you ask of me and then perish
there is no force on earth that can stop me from wishing for rain
and yet you still hold me above the waves
you still remember my name
and for this I am thankful   and for this
I am yours   I am

bringing joy to the table.
I am serving it to you with open palms   take this:
the last thing I have to give   take this:
a thousand rose hips boiled with brown sugar   take this:
my tongue before it ever said a lie, before it ever said a name
a kalimba tuned to the key of you whispering my name in a
crowded room   all of you
cracking your knuckles in the gulf
I will keep you from drowning just give me your hands
I will speak of a god at the edge of the ocean but I will always have
your face in mind.

I will bring joy to the table, with more chairs and more space
like a ribcage in which my lungs expand   and you
are the wind that fills them
you blow through the grass fields just enough to put out
the forest fire in my head

and I am thankful
I am not building a coffin from the tree
with our names carved in it
I am building a table.

A Rose, Growing at Sea

shed your skin. brace for impact. carry the whole sea on your
shoulders. laugh at the pain. laugh at the pain. participate. participate.
give yourself a reason to stay, like a garden, and nurture those flowers
until the end of time. sleep in the meadow of the flowers you lend
yourself to love because you believe in something more than just the
decay in your body, that if you could grow a home from the dirt and
the dust | then surely you deserved to live there.

THE WAY OUR FATHERS GO

I take after my father.
Although they are not together anymore,
my mother loves to remind me of the fact
that I inherited both his shoulders and his laugh

and eventually, she says, much to my dissent,
I will inherit his gut. His beast of a belly.

(and even though I beg to differ,
the fifty pounds I put on this year beg even more.)

There have always been miles between me and my father,
but it would be a lie to say he wasn't in my life.
The winds and valleys may have blown and rolled us away,
but two trees on either end of a forest still grow together.

I have learned very much from that man.
Enough to last a lifetime

(should a lifetime come).

He taught me how to love from a distance,
how to speak from afar and still be heard,
how to do so quietly,
how to love the same way.

He says, when the light turns green, you go.
He taught me how to go, even if you're not
sure where. He taught me how to lead the
same way.

(and then he went)
(and so did I)

I am convinced my father measures his bicep every day.
We would sit at the dinner table, and he would nudge my arm,
then he'd whisper to his muscles, *grow, grow grow*.
It was absolutely as pretentious as it sounds.

It took me a while to learn the blessing of growth
Whether it be my biceps or my belly,
or my understanding of this skin.
That inheriting his belly meant always having food on the table.
That speaking peacefully might mean living another day,
but it might not.
Because no matter the size of your belly, they may always see you
as a beast.

It took me a while to learn that we must learn from a distance,
on the off chance that we must love from the other side.

Because going when the light turns green meant always having the
means to do so.

So I will do so.
For my father,
who shined in my life from so far,
whose light made this skin feel worth something.
Who showed me that being a father is no easier
than being a sun.

And when my own forest grows,
and my own son rises,
I will show him how to go.

LIGHTHOUSING

A soft blue washes most nights away.
It crawls through the windows,
and I have been unslept for a while now.
Andrea, I know
you can have a war with yourself, but what does it mean to lose?
I want to battle-sprint forever,
but I don't want to get out of bed.

Some days grab me by the throat | they drag me out.
Every now and then, I go down without a fight.
They don't tell you
that the battles you don't pick | you always lose.
So tell me,
what happens to all the light bringers
when the fireworks die
How much is a crooked smile worth
when all my love is chipped tooth
and a long way down

What happens when you make a person your favorite color
The coffee smells strong, but it still works me | tired.
The navy blue is whispering
the afternoon to sleep.
In all my dreams | I choose to walk towards the light,
and everything is fading.
I am both the deep horizon | and the shore bringer.
Like each day is lighthousing | in all my dreams, the light leaves.
But every awakening
is a return to the bright | bright ricochet.
All the shades of blue applaud us.
Listen to them sing | *love*.
The day is their symphony | an ode to "life until now and
no further,"
they will sing us a new song tomorrow.
I know some days are only decided by the sounds that I wake up to.
Every day could be the last day
that I'll hear certain voices | I remember the last time I heard yours.

You can hurt anyone for the sake of love, except yourself.
Some of the sunsets you share with people will be underwhelming.
Most hands you hold will sweat.
I know most days feel like drowning, but surely
as the sand
will give to your fingers,
it still holds up the sea.
The light bringers never die.

The shore is a constant song.
The day is lighthousing
screaming out, "I love you, come closer!"
So go.

Run towards it you | bright chaser. Be the wall that
all your thoughts bounce off of
Kiss the navy away. Pull the soft blue in aggressively.
Every morning is a God-written letter to Death,
proclaiming, "I may not make it to tomorrow, but I will
always exist in this moment.
Today, I am a champion of having existed before.
You will never take that from me."

Golden Boy, Black Bird, in Unison

Golden boy sees his self in himself and
puts himself to sleep.
Golden sea eats black bird and
finally decides to sleep.
Golden boy goes to sleep on an empty stomach.

Golden boy vomits goodbyes into the black sea.
Black birds see golden boy, peck at their chests,
feed it to him, and go to sea on an empty stomach.
Golden boy sees his ghosts in himself and
puts his ghosts to sleep.

Golden ghosts see boy in the sea and
go to sleep on an empty stomach.
Black boy sees ghosts and
chews on them before he sleeps.
Golden boy sees black ghosts and
turns them into birds

Black birds dive head first into the golden sea.
Golden boy pecks at his chest and feeds it to his ghosts and goes
to sleep on an empty stomach.

Black boy, raw chest, open wound.
Black bird, open wings, neck deep—
Eucharist, if ever one could be,

but the ghosts, they sleep.
Finally, they sleep.

EARTHWATER

I've given up my dirty fingernails. | I've put away the digging
tools. | all the shovels | have returned to their roots and ore | I pull
myself out of the terrible progress I've made. lavender starts growing
| where I might have instead | I swear | I saw you eclipse the sun
| somewhere | between loving you then and missing you now | I
stopped burying myself alive.

WHERE THEY BURIED THE CROWNS

Won't they bury our crowns before we ever see gold
Won't they put bullets in our bellies before they ever put
bread by our feet?

Won't they grab us by our wrists before our hands
lead us to the tombstone before the water
the river before the bridge
the flood before the way home?

Won't they always close their palms as they deny us of our fists
    deny us the space to walk as they beg us for our boots
    rob us of our breath and demand we sit still
    ask us for forgiveness with their heels at our throat?

I have seen the beast when it feels cornered
how it points at our teeth as it sharpens its fangs
I have been called canine by a creature on all fours
I have been called savage by a drooling beast
I know what a shark can do when it tastes the blood
and won't they drink from our veins as if the cup runneth over?

as if it is a ritual of sorts
as if it is a godly thing to make someone bleed

but you and I know the truth
that before anything there was darkness and then God
asked darkness to open its eyes and God said it was good

and aren't we the first good thing
aren't we made of nothing
but holy

When they take our breath we still breathe
When they take our breath we still breathe

We still remember where they buried our crowns
We still remember the way to the river

We're still alive so we must keep going
We still have our fists we still have our wrists
We still know the way through the water
We still know the way back home
and we will never forget.

WE KNEEL TO BURY THE BODY

O saints of bare trees
the hands of
dead black bodies
reaching for the heavens

the heavens that we were promised.
the promised lands that have escaped us.
the slavery of our roots we have not yet abandoned.

O God of broken chains
of
adopting the fears of my ancestors
inheriting the scars of my father
and his and his and his

O Angels of the long silence
the song of
the black woman
the black transgender
the black queer

songs we
sing but do not listen to
listen to but not around
our fathers

O hair we pull on but cheeks we fail to kiss.
O fist we raise but hand we fail to lend to
the darker
the different
the not black enough

O Lord of bonnets and du-rag
of
coconut oil and ocean wave
thistle brush and do not drown
box braid and boxing ring
float like a twist out, swing like a weave

O Trayvon, saint of skittles and sweet tea
O Sandra, saint of say it with your chest
O Marshawn, saint of self-infliction and demon combat

Saint Alton of bootlegs and the Mississippi River
Jesus Christ of Charlottesville, of refugees and rebels against the state
Holy Ghost of Lynch Mobs
Father and Son of
the gone too soon | |

this prayer in | | your name
this prayer for | | all of you.

Rest, My Son

job well done.

Golden jaw,
smoking gun.

Never fight,
never run.

see you soon,
see you sun.

Rest, my son.
Job well done.

NAVY

One day, on a rainy day in march, five birds danced in a puddle in the parking spot next to my car. I came out later to watch them flying against the grain of the storm.

Sometimes, I wonder how my ghosts find their way into living things and then I remember:

I have opened my mouth to all of this. I drink from the same river that I drown in. I save myself from the same God I pray to. I am the swimmer and the sticks. I am all of it.

VIOLET

I hold you
in the softest spots
of my palms.

I speak your name
only in whispers.

I know you're out
there growing among
some wild wood
laying gently beneath
the feet of some silent creature.

GOLD

One day, there will be no difference. One day, I'll step into a shadow and feel warmth. I know there is a god waiting for me on the other side. With a simple explanation for all this. One day, all the bleeding will take a backseat to shining. No more baited breath. No more jury decisions. No more executioners. Just soft palms. One day, no more blood cells on the asphalt. One day, no more dead bees. One day, buzzing. One day, one day, one day.

I hope there is always gold waiting for you.

Bright

Gold.

Amen

I am the bone of my pen
    amen.

give me strength
to
    color the shutter of the earth
    pacify the temper of the ocean
    and other tearful things

give me all the suffer
I will burrow it in my chest plate
O, how heavy the burden of sacrifice
O, how the pen bleeds visceral.

The marrow of my bone is
enough to float through the
Sea of grief.

I will write you out of drowning
I will bring you back to shore.
    amen.

ACKNOWLEDGMENTS

My mother and father, of course. Write Bloody Publishing. Mic Check Poetry, Write About Now. Madi Mae, Bill, Amir. Jamal. Wave City Forever. Aryan, Darielle, Jharen. The Gully Princess, Ebony Stewart. Dwyane Wade and The Miami Heat. Lupa's Coffee. Austyn. Simon. Zach. iCon. Xavier CoolKid. Family. Pressure Gauge Press, The Harpoon Review, Wildness Journal, in which many of these poems were first given a home. The hundred-odd black birds who gather at the stoplight on Rock Prairie and Highway Six. That particular sunset from an Airbnb in the French Quarter in New Orleans that I spent alone on a set of green stairs in which I first thought of this book, in which I first imagined the end. The very first light that all of us came from. The love of my life, Bonnie.

ABOUT THE AUTHOR

Photo by Nicole Forsander

LINO ANUNCIACION is a Texas-transplant spoken word artist based in Bryan, Texas. He serves as President of Mic Check Poetry, a 501(c)3 non-profit poetry organization, and Director of Texas Grand Slam Poetry Festival, the largest individual poetry festival in Texas. Lino was the 2016 Mic Check Slam Champion, and took 2nd place at the 2017 Southwest Shootout Individual Slam. He is the author of *And Then You Begin to Sing*, as well as four other books. He works as the Senior Media Manager for Write Bloody Publishing. When he's not doing poems, he's making coffee at Lupa's Coffee in College Station, Texas and teaching poetry workshops in Houston, Texas for Writers in the Schools.

linothepoet.com

If You Like Lino Anunciacion, Lino Anunciacion Likes...

Counting Descent
Clint Smith

Favorite Daughter
Nancy Huang

Oh God Get Out Get Out
Bill Moran

Pecking Order
Nicole Homer

Strange Light
Derrick C. Brown

The Year of No Mistakes
Cristin O'Keefe Aptowicz

Write Bloody Publishing distributes and promotes great books of fiction, poetry and art every year. We are an independent press dedicated to quality literature and book design, with an office in Los Angeles, CA.

Our employees are authors and artists so we call ourselves a family. Our design team comes from all over America: modern painters, photographers and rock album designers create book covers we're proud to be judged by.

We publish and promote 8-12 tour-savvy authors per year. We are grass-roots, D.I.Y., bootstrap believers. Pull up a good book and join the family. Support independent authors, artists and presses.

**Want to know more about Write Bloody books, authors and events?
Join our maling list at**

www.writebloody.com

WRITE BLOODY BOOKS

CPSIA information can be obtained
at www.ICGtesting.com
Printed in the USA
FSHW01n2340041018

9 781938 912900